KU-239-891

Cooking
for
Dinner Parties

ORBIS · LONDON

Series Editor: Stella Henvey
Series Art Director: Grahame Dudley
Photographer: James Jackson
Stylist: Alison Williams
Home Economist: Janice Murfitt

First published in Great Britain by
Orbis Publishing Limited, London 1984 for
The Littlewoods Organization plc
Reprinted 1986 by Orbis Book Publishing Corporation Ltd.
A BPCC plc company

© 1984 Orbis Publishing Limited

All rights reserved. No part of this publication may be
reproduced, stored in a retrieval system, or transmitted, in
any form or by any means, electronic, mechanical,
photocopying, recording or otherwise, without the prior
permission of the publishers. Such permission, if granted,
is subject to a fee depending on the nature of the use.

Printed in Yugoslavia
ISBN 1-85155-052-6

CONTENTS

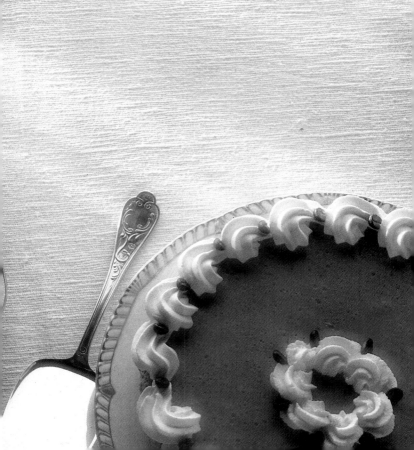

INTRODUCTION

Entertaining should be a pleasure, not a chore. These chapters provide mouthwatering dishes that don't take all day to prepare or cost a fortune. There are recipes for all sorts of occasions from stylish buffets to easy eats for relatives and close friends, from classy dinner parties to family celebrations.

To save last minute panic, plan wisely and shop in advance. Select a menu that offers a variety of textures and colours, choosing dishes you can manage and present well. If the main course needs last minute attention, pick a starter or dessert that can be made ahead or frozen.

FINISHING TOUCHES

The knack of successful entertaining is to make simple dishes look extra-special with carefully chosen garnishes and decorations. Here are some of the ways to add charisma to your cooking.

Crisp croûtons: use slices of slightly stale bread and trim off the crusts, then cut into small cubes or into fancy shapes with small cutters. Fry in butter, bacon fat or butter and oil until golden, stirring constantly. Drain on absorbent paper. Sprinkle over soups just before serving.

NOTES

Imperial and metric measurements are not exact equivalents, so follow one set only. Graded measuring spoons are used. Measurements are level unless otherwise specified.

The oven should be preheated to the recommended temperature.

Bake on the centre shelf unless otherwise directed.

Unless otherwise stated flour is white, oil is vegetable, herbs are fresh, vegetables and fruit are washed, trimmed and peeled and eggs are medium-large (EEC size 3)

Clever cucumber slices: score cucumber lengthways with a potato peeler, removing thin strips of skin, then cut into thin slices. (The slices will have a pretty, serrated edge). Float on top of clear soups and consommés, or use to garnish pâtés and mousses. Courgettes can be treated in the same way.

Spring onion tassels: make several slits in the stem end, without cutting through the bulb. Leave in iced water for about 1 hour to curl, then drain. Use to garnish salads, hamburgers and grills.

Julienne strips: cut raw or par-boiled vegetables into matchstick strips. Use to garnish soups.

Twists: cut wafer thin slices of unpeeled cucumber, lemon or orange. Make a cut from the centre of each slice to the edge. Twist the cut edges in opposite directions. Use to dress up open sandwiches, drinks, salads, mousses, moulds and cold cuts.

Butterflies: quarter slices of unpeeled cucumber, lemon or orange, then arrange in pairs with the points facing.

Parslied lemon wedges: cut a lemon lengthways into wedges, dip the end or centre edge into chopped parsley and serve with fish or seafood. Tomatoes can be treated in the same way.

Chocolate curls: shave long scrolls from the flat side of a block of chocolate with a sharp knife, or draw a potato peeler down the side of the block to make narrow curls.

Chocolate leaves: wash and dry well-shaped rose leaves. Using a fine paint brust, brush the veined underside of each leaf with melted chocolate cake covering taking care not to coat the otherside. Leave, chocolate side up, on a plate until set. Gently peel the leaf away from the chocolate. Store in an airtight container in the refrigerator for up to 2 weeks. You will need 4oz/100g chocolate covering to make 20 leaves.

Chopped nuts make a crunchy decoration for creamy desserts, ice cream, fruit compôtes and trifles. Toasted flaked almonds are excellent sprinkled over chocolate desserts and fruit fools.

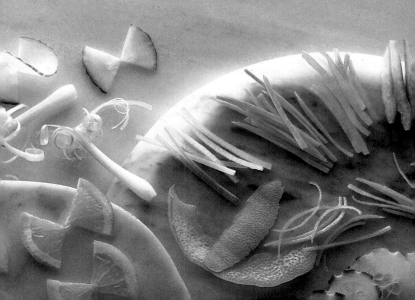

BUFFETS

SANGRIA

¼ cucumber, sliced
thinly pared rind of 1
   orange and 1 lemon
8oz/225g can peach slices
4tbls brandy
1¾ pints/1 litre red wine
18floz/500ml soda water

Place the cucumber and orange and lemon rinds in a large jug. Drain the peaches and add to the jug. Stir in the brandy and wine.

Just before serving, add the soda and 12 ice cubes. **Serves 20**

SPICED PARTY NIBBLES

2oz/50g butter
2×15oz/425g cans chick-
   peas, drained
8oz/225g blanched
   almonds
2tbls soft brown sugar
1tsp garam masala
1tsp ground cumin
1tsp ground turmeric
1tsp salt
½tsp black pepper
1tsp Worcestershire sauce

Melt the butter in a frying pan. Add the chick-peas and almonds and fry for 1 minute, or until golden brown.

Mix the sugar, spices, seasonings and sauce together. Add to pan and cook, stirring, for 1 minute.

Drain the spiced chick-peas and nuts on absorbent paper, then place in small serving dishes. **Serves 20**

TASTY BACON BITES

8 large slices white bread,
   crusts removed
2oz/50g soft tub
   margarine
5oz/150g Gouda cheese,
   grated
8oz/225g can pineapple
   slices, drained and
   chopped
8 rindless streaky bacon
   rashers
To garnish:
tomato wedges
parsley or coriander sprigs

Spread the bread with margarine and sprinkle with cheese and pineapple.

Stretch bacon slices flat with a knife, then cut across in half. Firmly roll up 1 prepared bread slice and cut in half. Wrap a bacon slice around each roll and secure with 2 wooden cocktail sticks.

Cut in half between the sticks to make 4 rolls. Make 28 more rolls, using remaining bacon and bread slices.

Place the rolls in the bottom of the grill pan and cook under a hot grill for about 4 minutes, turning once, until golden brown. Transfer to a serving dish and garnish. **Makes 32**

ROSÉ WINE CUP

8 cocktail cherries
8 strawberry slices
1 lemon, thinly sliced
4tbls kirsch
2 x 1¼ pint/70cl bottles
  rosé wine
1 pint/600ml lemonade
a few coriander leaves
extra strawberry slices

Put 1 cherry and 1 strawberry slice into a single compartment of an ice-cube tray. Repeat with the remaining cherries and strawberry slices. Fill each with water and freeze until solid.

Reserve 3 lemon slices; place the rest in a serving bowl with kirsch and wine.

Just before serving, add the lemonade, fruity ice cubes, coriander leaves and extra strawberry slices. Use reserved lemon slices to garnish the side of the bowl. **Serves 20**

COCKTAIL CHEESE BITES

4oz/100g processed
  cheese
2oz/50g blue cheese
8oz/225g cream cheese
2oz/50g margarine
2 spring onions, chopped
salt and black pepper
1tbls sweet paprika
2oz/50g chopped nuts
2tbls chopped parsley
To garnish:
1 lemon slice
parsley sprig
2 bay leaves

Grate the processed and blue cheeses and place in a mixing bowl. Add the cream cheese, margarine and spring onions, season and beat until well blended.

Divide into 48 pieces and roll each into a small ball. Roll half the balls in the paprika.

Mix the nuts with the parsley. Roll the remaining balls in the nut mixture. Garnish just before serving. **Makes 48**

SAVOURY PINWHEELS

Roll out 1 pastry sheet on a lightly floured surface to a 5 x 13in/13 x 33cm rectangle. Spread evenly with tomato purée and sprinkle with garlic salt.

Roll up firmly from 1 long side, to make a thin sausage, then cut into 25 equal slices.

Place the slices cut side down and well apart on a dampened baking sheet and brush lightly with egg. Bake in the oven preheated to 400F/200C/Gas 6 for about 10 minutes, or until crisp and pale golden. Transfer the tomato pinwheels to a wire rack to cool.

Roll out another pastry sheet to a rectangle as before, spread with yeast extract and sprinkle with sesame seeds. Roll up and slice, then glaze, bake and cool as for tomato pinwheels.

Roll out the third pastry sheet and spread with peanut butter; shape, glaze, bake and cool as for tomato pinwheels. Repeat with the last pastry sheet, spreading it with curry paste.

Arrange the pinwheels on a serving plate and garnish. **Makes 100**

4 sheets frozen puff
  pastry, defrosted, or
  12oz/350g frozen puff
  pastry, defrosted and
  quartered
1 tbls tomato purée
garlic salt
beaten egg, to glaze
1 tsp yeast extract
1 tsp sesame seeds
1 tbls crunchy peanut
  butter
1 tbls curry paste
watercress sprigs, to
  garnish

CABBAGE AND ORANGE SLAW

4 oranges
1½lb/700g white cabbage,
    finely shredded
2 large carrots, grated
1 onion, thinly sliced
4oz/100g seedless raisins
For the dressing:
5oz/150g natural yoghurt
2tbls orange juice
1tsp clear honey
salt and black pepper
To garnish:
3 orange slices
6 bay leaves

Thickly peel the oranges, removing every scrap of bitter white pith. Cut between the membrane to free the segments and remove any pips. Reserve 4 segments for garnish. Mix remaining segments with the cabbage, carrots, onion and raisins.

Place the yoghurt, orange juice and honey in a small bowl, season and whisk until blended. Pour the dressing over the salad and mix well.

Transfer the salad to a serving dish. Garnish with the reserved orange segments, the orange slices and bay leaves. **Serves 20**

AVOCADO MOUSSE

Place margarine, flour and chicken stock in a saucepan. Bring to boil over medium heat, whisking all the time, then simmer gently for 2 minutes.

Remove from the heat and stir in the dissolved gelatine, parsley, lemon zest and juice and mayonnaise.

Halve and stone the avocados. Mash the flesh and stir into sauce mixture. Season, then fold in the cream.

Rinse out 20 ramekin dishes or 2 x 2 pint/1 litre ring moulds. Divide mousse mixture between the dishes or moulds, cover and chill for 2-3 hours, until set.

Loosen the edges of each mousse, then turn out on to serving dishes and garnish. **Serves 20**

2oz/50g margarine
2oz/50g plain flour
1 pint/600ml chicken stock
2 sachets powdered gelatine, dissolved in 4tbls sherry
2tbls finely chopped parsley
grated zest and juice of 1 lemon
¾ pint/450ml mayonnaise
4 avocados
salt and black pepper
½ pint/300ml double cream, lightly whipped
To garnish:
4oz/100g peeled prawns
20 whole prawns
lemon slices, quartered
fennel sprigs

ITALIAN PASTA SALAD

10oz/275g pasta bows
salt
1 tbls olive oil
1 red pepper, chopped
1 green pepper, chopped
1 yellow pepper, chopped
3oz/75g black olives
3 pepperami salami, sliced
1 garlic clove, crushed
¼ pint/150ml mayonnaise
2 bay leaves, to garnish

Cook the pasta bows in plenty of boiling salted water for about 10 minutes, or until just tender. Drain, turn into a bowl and stir in the oil.

Add the peppers, olives, salami and mix well. Mix the garlic and mayonnaise, then stir into the salad.

Transfer to a serving bowl and garnish. **Serves 20**

MIXED BEAN PLATTER

12oz/350g French beans
1lb/450g frozen broad beans
salt
2 heads chicory
15oz/425g can red kidney beans, drained and rinsed
6 celery stalks, sliced
½ cucumber, thinly sliced
oil and vinegar, to serve

Cook the French beans and broad beans, separately, in boiling salted water for 3-5 minutes, until tender but still crisp. Drain and rinse under cold water, then cool.

Separate the chicory into leaves and arrange on a serving dish. Add the French beans, kidney beans and broad beans, arranged in neat bands, then add the celery and cucumber slices.

Serve with oil and vinegar. **Serves 20**

NUTTY BROWN RICE

Cook rice in plenty of boiling salted water for about 30 minutes, or until tender. Drain and rinse under cold water, then drain again thoroughly.

Place rice, nuts and sweetcorn in a mixing bowl.

Quarter and core the apples. Cut 4 thin slices of apple, dip in lemon juice and reserve for garnish. Chop remaining apples, add to the lemon juice in a bowl and mix well.

Strain the lemon juice from apples into a small bowl. Whisk in oil and mustard and season to taste.

Stir chopped apples and lemon dressing into rice mixture. Transfer to a serving bowl and garnish. **Serves 20**

12oz/350g brown rice
salt
2oz/50g salted peanuts
2oz/50g unsalted cashew nuts, chopped
7oz/200g can sweetcorn kernels, drained
3 red-skinned apples
4tbls lemon juice
6tbls oil
½tsp made mustard
black pepper
parsley sprigs, to garnish

PINK PÂTÉ

4oz/100g sliced smoked
   salmon
3 x 8oz/225g cans
   mackerel in brine,
   drained, bones removed
6oz/175g butter, melted
grated zest and juice of 1
   small lemon
4tbls sherry
1tbls tomato purée
4oz/100g fresh white
   breadcrumbs
salt and black pepper
To garnish:
cucumber slices
lemon slices and twists
fennel sprigs

Line a 1lb/500g loaf tin with cling film. Line the base and long sides with salmon slices, trimming them to fit. Reserve the trimmings.

Place the mackerel in bowl and mash well. Add the butter, lemon zest and juice, sherry and tomato purée and beat until smoothly blended. Stir in the breadcrumbs and season.

Carefully spoon the mixture into the lined tin and level the surface. Cover with cling film and chill for 3-4 hours.

Turn the pâté out on to a serving dish and remove the cling film. Roll up small strips of reserved salmon trimmings to make 'flowers' and use to garnish the pâté together with the cucumber, lemon and fennel.

Makes 20 slices

PARTY SANDWICH STACKS

Butter the bread. Spread 4 slices of brown bread evenly with pâté. Cover each with a slice of white bread, buttered side down. Spread the tops with butter.

Mix the eggs with the mustard and cress and mayonnaise, then season. Spread the egg mixture evenly over the top of each sandwich, then place a brown slice on top, buttered side down. Spread the tops with butter.

Beat the taramasalata with the cream cheese and spread over the sandwich stacks. Place the remaining white bread on top, buttered sides down. Wrap each stack in cling film and chill until required.

Cut the crusts off each stack, then spread the sides with some of the cheese spread. Coat 2 opposite sides of each stack with chopped peanuts, then coat the remaining sides with chopped parsley. Spread the tops of the stacks with the rest of the cheese spread.

Place the stacks on a serving plate and garnish. To serve, cut each stack into 4 slices, then cut each slice into 4 pieces. **Makes 64 pieces**

softened butter, for spreading
8 large slices white bread
8 large slices brown bread
4oz/100g duck pâté
3 hard-boiled eggs, chopped
2tbls mustard and cress
1tbls mayonnaise
salt and black pepper
2oz/50g taramasalata
2oz/50g cream cheese
8oz/225g jar cheese spread
4oz/100g salted peanuts, chopped
6tbls chopped parsley
To garnish:
1oz/25g salted peanuts
3 radishes, thinly sliced
parsley sprigs

TURKEY STROGANOFF

10lb/4.5kg oven-ready
  turkey, defrosted if
  frozen
2oz/50g margarine
2tbls oil
8 rindless streaky bacon
  rashers, chopped
4 onions, thinly sliced
1½lb/700g button
  mushrooms, sliced
3tbls cornflour
6tbls sherry
¾ pint/450ml chicken
  stock
2tbls tomato purée
salt and black pepper
¾ pint/450ml single
  cream
boiled rice, to serve
To garnish:
triangles of fried bread
parsley sprigs

Remove the flesh from turkey carcass and bones and cut it into thin strips.

Heat margarine and oil in a large frying pan. Add bacon and turkey and fry briskly for 4-5 minutes. Remove from the pan with a slotted spoon.

Add onions and mushrooms to pan, cover and cook briskly for 2-3 minutes. Blend cornflour with sherry and stir into pan with the stock and purée. Bring to the boil, stirring, and simmer for 2 minutes. Add turkey and bacon and season.

Stir in the cream and heat through without boiling.

Pour into a serving dish and garnish. Serve at once, with rice. **Serves 20**

CELEBRATION PORK

4lb/1.75kg loin of pork,
  boned
4oz/100g dried apricots,
  chopped
1 onion, finely chopped
8oz/225g fresh
  breadcrumbs
2tbls chopped parsley
1tsp finely chopped sage
grated zest and juice of 1
  lemon
2 eggs, beaten
salt and black pepper
1 sachet powdered
  gelatine, dissolved in
  3tbls water
¼ pint/150ml chicken
  stock
¼ pint/150ml
  mayonnaise
To garnish:
dried apricots
spring onion stalks
fennel sprigs

Place pork, bone side up, on a board. Mix apricots, onion, breadcrumbs, herbs, lemon zest and juice and eggs. Season, then spread over pork.

Roll pork up firmly and secure with string; wrap in foil and place in a roasting tin. Bake in the oven pre-heated to 375F/190C/Gas 5 for 2 hours, or until tender. Slit foil open and leave pork to cool, then remove string and skin.

Stir the dissolved gelatine into the stock. Reserve 1tbls stock. Beat remaining stock into mayonnaise and allow to thicken to a coating consistency, then pour over pork. Leave to set.

Garnish with apricots, onion stalks and fennel, dipping the pieces in the reserved and melted stock before arranging on the pork. **Serves 20**

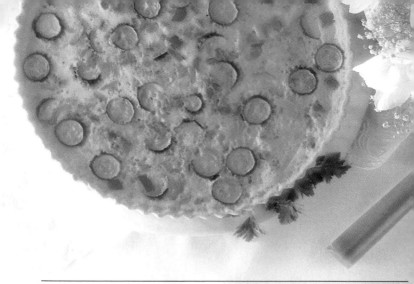

FIESTA QUICHE

12oz/350g shortcrust
  pastry, defrosted if
  frozen
Filling and garnish:
1 tbls oil
4 rindless streaky bacon
  rashers, chopped
2 courgettes, thinly sliced
1 small red pepper, seeded
  and chopped
1 onion, chopped
3 eggs
¼ pint/150ml single
  cream
¼ pint/150ml milk
1 tsp finely chopped
  oregano or ¼ tsp dried
  oregano
salt and black pepper
parsley sprigs, to garnish

Roll out the pastry on a lightly floured surface to an 11in/28cm circle and use to line a 10in/25cm fluted flan tin with a loose base. Trim excess pastry, then prick the base with a fork.

Line the pastry case with greaseproof paper or foil and weight down with baking beans. Bake in the oven pre-heated to 400F/200C/Gas 6 for 15 minutes. Lift out the paper and beans.

Lower the oven heat to 325F/160C/Gas 3.

To make the filling, heat the oil in a frying pan, add bacon and fry briskly until brown. Stir in courgettes, pepper and onion and fry for 2-3 minutes, until softened. Spoon the vegetable mixture into the pastry case and spread evenly.

Beat eggs, cream, milk and herbs; season and pour into the pastry case.

Bake for about 30 minutes, or until the filling is set. Cool the quiche in the tin, then transfer to a serving dish and garnish. **Makes 10-12 slices**

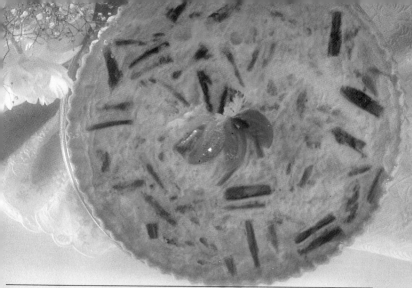

ASPARAGUS QUICHE

Roll out the pastry on a lightly floured surface to an 11in/28cm circle and use to line a 10in/25cm fluted flan tin with a loose base. Trim excess pastry, then prick the base with a fork.

Line the pastry case with greaseproof paper or foil and weight down with baking beans. Bake in the oven preheated to 400F/200C/Gas 6 for 15 minutes. Lift out paper and beans.

Lower the oven heat to 325F/160C/Gas 3.

To make the filling, arrange the cheese slices and asparagus spears over the pastry base. Beat the eggs with the cream, milk and mustard; season and pour into the pastry case.

Bake for about 30 minutes, or until the filling is set. Cool the quiche in the tin, then transfer to a serving dish and garnish. **Makes 10-12 slices**

12oz/350g shortcrust pastry, defrosted if frozen
For the filling:
4oz/100g Gruyère cheese, thinly sliced
10½oz/290g can asparagus cut spears, drained
3 eggs
¼ pint/150ml single cream
¼ pint/150ml milk
¼tsp made mustard
salt and black pepper
To garnish:
3 tomato wedges
parsley sprig

MINSTREL SLICE

6oz/175g self-raising flour
1tsp baking powder
6oz/175g margarine or
  butter, softened
6oz/175g caster sugar
3 eggs
For the topping:
¼ pint/150ml double
  cream, stiffly whipped
4oz/100g black grapes,
  halved and seeded
4oz/100g white grapes,
  halved and seeded
juice of 1 orange
1tsp arrowroot

Sift the flour and baking powder into a mixing bowl. Add the margarine, sugar and eggs. Beat together with a wooden spoon for 2 minutes or with a hand-held electric whisk for 1 minute.

Turn the mixture into a greased and lined 9 x 13in/23 x 33cm Swiss roll tin. Bake in the oven preheated to 325F/160C/Gas 3 for about 30 minutes, or until springy to the touch. Turn out on to a wire rack, remove paper and leave until cold.

Cut the cake lengthways in half. Spread each piece with cream. Top 1 cake with rows of white grapes and the other cake with black grapes.

Blend the arrowroot and orange juice in a small pan and boil for 1 minute. Allow to cool, then brush over grapes.

To serve, cut each cake into 20 thin slices. **Makes 40 slices**

CHOCOLATE LEAF CAKE

3oz/75g margarine,
  melted
3tbls melted chocolate
10oz/275g digestive
  biscuits, crushed
Filling and decoration:
4oz/100g butter, diced
4½oz/135g tablet lemon
  jelly, cut into cubes
grated zest and juice of 1
  small lemon
8oz/225g low fat cream
  cheese
¾ pint/450ml whipping
  cream
28 chocolate leaves (see
  p5)

Mix the margarine, melted chocolate and biscuits together. Spoon into a 1in/2.5cm deep, 7 x 11in/18 x 28cm tin lined with non-stick baking paper and press evenly over the base.

To make the filling, put the butter and jelly in a small saucepan and stir over low heat until melted, then pour into a blender. Add the lemon zest and juice, cheese and ¼ pint/150ml cream and blend until smooth. Pour the mixture over biscuit base and chill for 2-3 hours, until set.

Lift the cheesecake out of tin and peel back lining paper, then cut into 28 squares. Whip remaining cream until soft peaks form. Pipe or spoon a swirl of cream on each square and top with a chocolate leaf. **Makes 28**

ORANGE MERINGUES

Place meringues on a flat surface.

Grate the zest from 1 of the oranges and reserve. Thickly peel the oranges, removing every scrap of white pith. Cut between the membranes to free the segments and remove any pips. Drain the segments and reserve.

Whip the cream with the orange zest and milk until it stands in soft peaks. Pipe or spoon a swirl of cream into each nest. Decorate with reserved orange segments. Keep in a cool place until ready to serve. **Makes 20**

20 meringue nests, home-made or bought
Filling and decoration:
3 oranges
½ pint/300ml double or whipping cream
2 tbls milk

Informal Entertaining

CONTINENTAL STARTER

6 slices honey roast ham
6 slices chicken roll
6 slices Danish salami
6 slices French garlic
  sausage
6 slices smoked gammon
12 slices dry cured beef
To garnish:
12 lemon twists
24 black olives
rosemary sprigs

Fold each slice of ham, chicken roll, salami and garlic sausage in half and divide between 6 small serving plates, arranging them in a neat row.

Pleat the smoked gammon and place at the end of each row of meat. Ruffle the cured beef and arrange 2 slices on each plate.

Garnish each platter with 2 lemon twists, 4 olives and rosemary sprigs.
Serves 6

FRENCH ONION SOUP

1 tbls olive oil
1 lb/450g onions, thinly
  sliced
2 pints/1 litre beef stock
salt and black pepper
To serve:
6 slices French bread
1 tbls French mustard
3oz/75g Gruyère cheese,
  grated

Heat the oil in a large saucepan. Add onions and fry over moderate heat until golden brown, stirring occasionally.

Add the stock and bring to the boil, then cover and simmer for 20 minutes. Season to taste.

Arrange the bread on a grill rack and toast on one side only until golden brown. Turn the bread over and spread the untoasted sides with mustard, then sprinkle with grated cheese. Return to the grill and cook until the cheese melts.

To serve, ladle the soup into warmed individual bowls and place a slice of toasted cheese bread in the centre of each portion. **Serves 6**

FISH CHOWDER

1 tbls oil
4 rindless streaky bacon
  rashers, chopped
1 onion, thinly sliced
2 courgettes, thinly sliced
4 floury potatoes, diced
½ pint/300ml chicken
  stock
1 pint/600ml milk
1 bay leaf
1 tbls finely chopped
  parsley
black pepper
11oz/300g can sweetcorn
  kernels, drained
1lb/450g smoked haddock
  fillets, chopped

Heat the oil in a large saucepan, add the bacon and fry until browned. Stir in the onion and courgettes and cook for 2 minutes, until softened.

Add potatoes, stock, milk, bay leaf, parsley and black pepper to taste. Bring to the boil, stirring, then cover and simmer gently for 10 minutes.

Stir in the sweetcorn and haddock and simmer gently for a further 5 minutes, or until the fish is cooked. Check the seasoning, then ladle into a warmed serving dish. Serve at once.
Serves 6

PEAR APPETIZER

2oz/50g low fat cream
  cheese
2oz/50g Dolcelatte cheese
2 tbls mayonnaise
3 tbls single cream
salt and black pepper
3 pears
2 tbls lemon juice
To garnish:
curly endive leaves
3 celery stalks, sliced
3 radishes, sliced
quartered lemon slices

Beat the cheeses together until smoothly blended. Stir in the mayonnaise and cream, then season to taste.

Peel, quarter and core 1 pear. Cut each quarter into 2 slices and quickly brush with lemon juice to prevent them turning brown. Prepare the remaining pears in the same way.

Spread some of the cheese mixture over the centre of 6 small serving plates. Arrange 4 pear slices on top of each portion and garnish with endive and celery. Pipe or spoon the remaining cheese mixture on to each plate and garnish with radish slices and lemon quarters. **Serves 6**

HERBY GARLIC ROLLS

Beat the cheese and butter together until soft and creamy.

Cut each roll diagonally into thick slices, without cutting through the base. Gently fan open the slices and spread with the cheese mixture.

Wrap each roll in foil and seal well. Place in the oven preheated to 400F/200C/Gas 6 for about 10 minutes, or until the rolls are hot and the cheese spread has melted and soaked into the crumb. Unwrap and serve at once.

Serves 6

4oz/100g soft cheese with garlic and herbs
4oz/100g butter, softened
6 assorted bread rolls

SALAD NICOISE

8oz/225g French beans
2 hard-boiled eggs
2 tomatoes
7oz/200g can tuna in oil,
    drained
1 small iceberg lettuce
½ cucumber, thinly sliced
1 onion, sliced into rings
1 green pepper, seeded and
    sliced into rings
¾oz/50g can anchovy
    fillets, drained
2oz/50g black olives
For the dressing:
3tbls olive oil
1tbls wine vinegar
1tbls chopped parsley
½tsp Dijon mustard
½tsp caster sugar
salt and black pepper

Cook the beans in boiling salted water for 2 minutes; drain and rinse under cold water, then cool.

Cut the eggs and tomatoes into quarters. Flake the tuna into bite-sized pieces and tear the lettuce leaves into small pieces.

Cover a serving dish with lettuce leaves. Arrange the cucumber slices, egg wedges, French beans, tomato wedges, onion rings, pepper rings and tuna fish decoratively over lettuce. Arrange the anchovy fillets and olives in the centre.

To make the dressing, whisk the oil, vinegar, parsley, mustard and sugar together and season to taste.

Just before serving, pour the dressing over the salad. **Serves 6**

SPANISH RICE

Heat the oil in a saucepan. Add the flaked almonds and fry until golden, then drain on absorbent paper. Add the onion and fry for 2 minutes until softened, then stir in the tomato purée, rice, salt and 1¼ pints/700ml water. Bring to the boil, stirring, then cover and cook for about 10 minutes, or until rice has absorbed all the water and is tender. Leave to cool.

Toss the mushroom slices in the lemon juice, then add to rice with prawns and peas and mix well. Transfer to a serving bowl.

Halve the tomato slices. Remove the shells from tail end of prawns. Garnish the rice with the tomatoes, prawns and bay leaves. **Serves 6**

1 tbls oil
2oz/50g flaked almonds
1 onion, finely chopped
2 tbls tomato purée
6oz/175g long-grain rice
1 tsp salt
*4oz/100g button
  mushrooms, sliced*
1 tbls lemon juice
*6oz/175g peeled prawns,
  defrosted if frozen*
4oz/100g cooked peas
To garnish:
2 tomatoes, thinly sliced
2 whole prawns
2 bay leaves

SPEEDY RATATOUILLE

1 large aubergine, sliced
3 courgettes, sliced
salt
4 tbls olive oil
3 onions, sliced
2 red peppers, seeded and
   sliced
1 green pepper, seeded and
   sliced
4 large tomatoes, skinned
   and sliced
1 garlic clove, crushed
1 tbls finely chopped
   coriander leaves
black pepper

Layer the aubergine and courgette slices in a colander, sprinkling salt over each layer. Cover with a plate and leave to drain over a bowl.

Heat the oil in a large heavy-based saucepan, add the onions and cook for 2 minutes until softened, stirring occasionally.

Press as much liquid as possible out of the aubergines and courgettes, then add to the pan with the peppers. Stir over medium heat for 2 minutes, then add the tomatoes, garlic and coriander. Season with pepper and bring to the boil. Cover and cook gently for about 10 minutes, or until all vegetables are tender.

Transfer the ratatouille to a warmed serving dish and serve at once. **Serves 6**

CARROTS WITH ONIONS

Cook the carrots and onions in separate pans of boiling salted water until just tender. Allow about 8 minutes for the carrots and 10 minutes for the onions. Drain and keep warm in separate dishes.

Melt the butter in a saucepan, add the sugar and ¼ pint/150ml water. Heat gently, stirring occasionally, until sugar has dissolved. Bring to the boil and boil briskly, without stirring, for about 1 minute or until syrupy. Remove from the heat.

Add the carrots to the syrup and turn them until evenly coated, then transfer to a warmed serving dish.

Add the onions to the syrup and turn carefully to coat, then arrange in the dish with carrots. Garnish and serve at once. **Serves 6**

12 even-sized carrots
12 small onions
salt
2oz/50g butter
2oz/50g caster sugar
coriander leaves or
*   parsley sprigs, to*
*   garnish*

CIDER APPLE CUP

1¾ pints/1 litre strong
  cider
1 stick cinnamon
3 cloves
2tbls clear honey
juice of 1 orange
1 red-skinned apple
1tbls lemon juice
18floz/500ml soda water
To garnish:
orange slices
mint leaves

Pour ½ pint/300ml cider into a saucepan. Add the spices and honey. Bring to the boil, then leave until cold.

Strain spiced cider into a glass bowl. Add remaining cider and orange juice. Quarter, core and slice the apple, then toss in lemon juice and add to the bowl.

Just before serving, stir in the soda and 10 ice cubes. Garnish and serve.
Serves 6

CHIVE BAKED POTATOES

6 baking potatoes, in their
  skins
¼ pint/150ml soured
  cream
3tbls chopped chives
salt and black pepper

Prick potatoes well with a fork and place on a baking tray. Bake in the oven preheated to 375F/190C/Gas 5 for about 1 hour, or until tender.

Cut tops off potatoes. Scoop out the flesh into a bowl, leaving the shells intact. Reserve 2tbls of the soured cream; add the rest to the bowl with 2tbls chives. Season and mash until smooth. Spoon the mixture back into potato shells. Top with reserved cream and sprinkle with remaining chives.
Serves 6

BACON BAKED POTATOES

6 baking potatoes, in their
  skins
6 rindless streaky bacon
  rashers
3oz/75g button
  mushrooms, chopped
2oz/50g butter or
  margarine
salt and black pepper
To garnish:
mushroom slices
parsley sprigs

Bake potatoes as above recipe.

Cut 2 bacon rashers across into 3 pieces. Roll up each piece and thread on to wooden cocktail sticks. Grill the bacon rolls and the remaining rashers for 5 minutes, turning once. Reserve.

Cut the tops off the potatoes. Scoop out the flesh into a bowl, leaving the shells intact. Chop the grilled bacon rashers and add to bowl with the mushrooms. Season and mash well. Spoon the mixture back into the potato shells. Garnish with mushrooms, parsley and bacon rolls and serve.
Serves 6

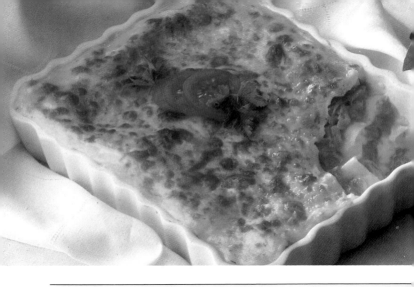

SMOKY PASTA LAYER

2oz/50g margarine
2oz/50g plain flour
1 pint/600ml milk
1 tbls chopped parsley
1 egg, beaten
2 hard-boiled eggs,
　chopped
6oz/175g Cheddar
　cheese, grated
salt and black pepper
12 sheets no need to
　pre-cook lasagne
6 tomatoes, skinned,
　seeded and chopped
1lb/450g kipper fillets,
　flaked.
To garnish:
tomato slices
coriander or parsley sprigs

Whisk the margarine, flour and milk together in a saucepan. Bring to the boil, stirring, then simmer for 2 minutes.

Remove from the heat and stir in the parsley, beaten egg, chopped eggs and 4oz/100g cheese. Season to taste.

Spread one-quarter of the cheese sauce over the base of a shallow, square ovenproof dish and cover with 4 sheets of lasagne. Scatter over half the chopped tomatoes and flaked kippers.

Spoon one-third of the remaining sauce on top, then cover with 4 sheets of lasagne. Add the rest of the tomatoes and kippers and top with half the remaining sauce. Arrange the last 4 sheets of lasagne on top and spread with the remaining sauce. Scatter the remaining cheese on top.

Bake in the oven preheated to 375F/190C/Gas 5 for about 45 minutes, or until lasagne is tender when pierced with a knife. Garnish and serve.
Serves 6

ALL SEASONS PIZZA

Heat 1tbls oil in a saucepan, add onions and basil and cook for 3 minutes, stirring occasionally. Stir in the tomatoes and purée. Boil briskly until thickened, season and leave to cool.

Place bread mix in a bowl, add 6½fl oz/185ml tepid water and mix to a dough. Turn out and knead for 5 minutes, then cover and leave for 5 minutes.

Cut the dough in half. Roll out each piece to a 10in/25cm round and place on 1-2 greased baking sheets.

Brush the dough rounds lightly with some of the remaining oil. Spread the tomato mixture over the top of each round, to within ½in/1cm of edges. Sprinkle with grated Mozzarella. Bake in the oven preheated to 425F/220C/ Gas 7 for about 15 minutes or until dough is lightly browned.

Remove the pizza from the oven and top each with mushrooms, garlic sausage, triangles of cheese, gherkins, anchovies and olives. Brush generously with oil and return to the oven for 5 minutes. Serve hot, cut into wedges.
Serves 8

3tbls oil
2 large onions, sliced
1tsp chopped basil
8oz/225g can tomatoes
2tbls tomato purée
salt and black pepper
10oz/280g packet white bread mix
8oz/225g Mozzarella cheese, grated
4oz/100g button mushrooms, sliced
12 slices garlic sausage, quartered
4 slices processed cheese, cut into triangles
2 gherkins, sliced
12 anchovy fillets, cut into strips
8 black olives, stoned and chopped

TWO-WAY PITTA POCKETS

3 pitta breads, cut in half
Mince filling:
1 tbls oil
1 onion, finely chopped
6oz/175g minced beef
8oz/225g can tomatoes
1 tbls tomato purée
salt and black pepper
mustard, for spreading
6 bay leaves
Salad filling:
mayonnaise, for spreading
6 lettuce leaves
12 cucumber slices
6 tomato slices
6 green pepper rings
3 slices Danish salami
3 slices smoked cheese
watercress sprigs

Prepare the mince filling: heat oil in a saucepan. Add the onion and fry for 2 minutes, then stir in the beef and fry over high heat until brown. Add tomatoes and tomato purée. Bring to the boil, then cover and simmer gently for 20 minutes. Season to taste.

Make the salad pittas: spread the insides of 3 of the pitta pockets with mayonnaise. Divide the lettuce, cucumber, tomato, pepper, salami and cheese between the pockets and garnish with watercress.

Make the mince pittas: spread the insides of the remaining pitta pockets lightly with mustard. Fill with the cooked mince and garnish.

Serve at once. **Serves 6**

DANISH OPEN SANDWICHES

8 lettuce leaves
8 slices pumpernickel,
  buttered
For the toppings:
3oz/75g peeled prawns,
  defrosted if frozen
2 tbls coleslaw
6 cucumber slices
4 lemon twists
3oz/75g Danish Blue
  cheese
4 grapes
1 radish, thinly sliced
2 tomato wedges
1 rollmop herring
6 onion rings
10 apple slices, tossed in
  lemon juice
4 black olives
2 slices dry cured beef
6 slices smoked gammon
3 stuffed olives, sliced
2 orange slices

Place a lettuce leaf on each slice of pumpernickel.

Divide prawns, coleslaw and cucumber slices attractively between 2 of the slices. Garnish each with a lemon twist.

Cut the cheese in half. Place a piece of cheese on 2 of the remaining pumpernickel slices and garnish with the grapes, radish slices, tomato wedges and a lemon twist.

Cut the herring in half and arrange on 2 of the other slices with onion rings, apple slices and black olives.

Divide the beef and gammon between the remaining pumpernickel and garnish with stuffed olives and orange twists. Serve as soon as possible.
Makes 8

CHINESE CHICKEN

3 chicken breasts, boned
4 carrots
4 courgettes
2 onions
1 red pepper, seeded
1 green pepper, seeded
1oz/25g butter
2tbls oil
1 garlic clove, crushed
¼ pint/150ml chicken
   stock
1tsp soy sauce
1tsp cornflour
salt and black pepper
bay leaves, to garnish

Cut the chicken meat, carrots and courgettes into matchstick strips. Thinly slice the onions and peppers.

Heat the butter and oil in a large frying pan. Add chicken and fry over high heat for 2 minutes, stirring constantly. Remove from the pan with a slotted spoon and reserve.

Add the carrots and onions to the pan and stir-fry for 2 minutes, stirring occasionally. Stir in the peppers and garlic and stir-fry for a further 2 minutes.

Return chicken to pan. Add the stock and bring to the boil. Blend soy sauce and cornflour with 1tbls water, then stir into the pan. Bring to the boil and simmer for 1 minute. Season to taste.

Serve at once, garnished with bay leaves. **Serves 6**

TASTY TAGLIATELLE

Cook the tagliatelle in plenty of boiling salted water until just tender: about 5 minutes if fresh and 15 minutes if dried. Drain well.

Meanwhile, beat the eggs with cream, half the cheese and pepper to taste.

Heat the oil in a large frying pan, add the bacon and fry for about 3 minutes until browned. Add the drained tagliatelle and stir over low heat for 1 minute.

Remove from the heat, pour in the egg mixture and stir until eggs thicken.

Serve at once, sprinkled with the remaining cheese and garnished with parsley and tomato. **Serves 4**

1¼lb/500g fresh or 8oz/
   225g dried tagliatelle
salt
4 eggs
2tbls single cream
2oz/50g grated Parmesan
   cheese
black pepper
1tbls oil
6 rindless streaky bacon
   rashers, chopped
To garnish:
parsley
tomato slices

CURRIED CHICKEN SALAD

5oz/150g natural yoghurt
1 tbls curry paste
1 tbls mango chutney
½ pint/300ml mayonnaise
1½lb/700g cooked
  chicken meat
salt and black pepper
To serve:
¼tsp turmeric
1lb/450g cold boiled rice
1 lemon twist
coriander leaves

Stir the yoghurt, curry paste and chutney into the mayonnaise, mixing well. Season to taste.

Cut the chicken into bite-sized pieces and add to the curried mayonnaise, turning the pieces to coat them evenly.

Add the turmeric to the rice and stir until evenly coloured.

Serve the curried chicken with the coloured rice, garnished with the lemon and coriander. **Serves 6**

SPICY LAMB PIES

1 tbls oil
1 onion, finely chopped
1 garlic clove, crushed
12oz/350g lamb fillet,
  minced
2 tsp curry paste
½tsp turmeric
2 tsp lemon juice
2 tbls single cream or milk
salt and black pepper
1½-1¾lb/700-800g
  shortcrust pastry,
  defrosted if frozen
beaten egg, to glaze

Heat the oil in a saucepan. Add the onion, garlic and lamb and fry for about 3 minutes, until browned.

Stir in the curry paste, turmeric and lemon juice and cook gently for 2 minutes. Remove from the heat, stir in cream and season to taste. Leave to cool.

Thinly roll out half the pastry and cut into 12 rounds with a 4in/10cm cutter. Use the rounds to line 12 deep patty tins.

Spoon the lamb mixture into the pastry cases and smooth each surface. Brush the pastry edges lightly with water.

Roll out the remaining pastry and cut into 12 rounds with a 3in/8cm cutter, reserving the trimmings. Place the rounds on top of the filling. Press pastry edges together to seal and crimp them.

Brush the lids with egg, then pierce the top with a knife. Make decorations from pastry trimmings, place on top of each pie and brush with egg.

Bake in the oven preheated to 350F/180C/Gas 4 for about 35 minutes, or until the pastry is cooked and golden brown. Serve warm. **Makes 12**

LITTLE SUMMER PUDDINGS

6oz/175g granulated
  sugar
8oz/225g redcurrants,
  stripped from stalks
8oz/225g strawberries,
  hulled
8oz/225g raspberries
4oz/100g gooseberries,
  topped and tailed
12 large slices white
  bread, crusts removed
whipped cream, to
  decorate (optional)

Place the sugar in a saucepan with ¼ pint/150ml water. Heat gently, stirring, until sugar has dissolved.

Reserve a little fruit for decoration. Add the remaining fruit to the pan, cover and cook gently for 5 minutes. Remove from the heat.

Have ready 6 ramekins. Flatten the bread slices with a rolling pin. Using a cutter the same diameter as the ramekins, cut out 12 rounds of bread. Place 1 bread round in base of each dish. Line the sides with bread, making sure there are no gaps.

Divide the cooked fruit between the bread-lined dishes, then fill to the top with juice. Reserve remaining juice. Cover with remaining bread rounds, pressing down gently to absorb the juice. Leave to stand for 30 minutes.

Cover the top of each pudding with cling film, then stand the dishes on a plate to catch any juice. Place a light weight on top of each pudding and chill overnight.

To serve: uncover puddings and loosen sides with a knife, then turn out on to individual plates. Spoon reserved juice over each pudding and decorate.
Serves 6

PEACH YOGHURT FLAN

Melt the margarine with the syrup in a saucepan. Remove from the heat and stir in the crushed biscuits, mixing well.

Spoon the biscuit mixture into a loose-based 10in/25cm fluted flan tin and press firmly and evenly over the base and up the sides. Set aside.

Dissolve the jelly in 8fl oz/250ml boiling water. Pour into a bowl; cool, then chill until thickened but not set.

Reserve 8 peach slices for decoration; finely chop the rest and scatter over the base of the biscuit case.

Whisk the yoghurt into the almost set jelly, then quickly pour into the biscuit case. Chill for 1 hour, or until the filling is set.

Remove the sides of the tin and transfer the flan to a serving plate. Lightly whip the cream, if using, and pipe or spoon around the edge of the flan. Decorate with the reserved peach slices. **Serves 6**

4oz/100g margarine, diced
2tbls golden syrup
10oz/275g ginger biscuits, crushed
4¾oz/135g peach flavour jelly, cut into cubes
8oz/225g can sliced peaches, drained
2 x 5oz/150g cartons peach melba or raspberry yoghurt
¼ pint/150ml double or whipping cream, to decorate (optional)

ICE CREAM SUNDAES

4¾oz/135g strawberry
flavour jelly, cut into
cubes
4¾oz/135g greengage or
lime flavour jelly, cut
into cubes
18 scoops vanilla ice
cream
8oz/225g strawberries,
hulled and sliced
¼ pint/150ml whipping
cream, lightly whipped
2 kiwi fruit, sliced
2 tbls crunchy topping
12 wafers or other crisp
biscuits

Dissolve strawberry jelly in ¼ pint/
150ml boiling water. Make up to 1 pint/
600ml with cold water, then pour into a
shallow dish. Prepare greengage jelly in
the same way. Leave to set.

Meanwhile, chill 6 tall sundae
glasses.

To make the sundaes, coarsely break
up each jelly with a fork. Put 1tbls
strawberry jelly into the bottom of each
glass and top with 1 scoop ice cream.
Add 1tbls strawberries, then 2 scoops
ice cream and 1tbls greengage jelly.
Pipe or spoon a large swirl of cream on
top. Decorate with kiwi fruit and
strawberry slices. Sprinkle cream with
crunchy topping.

Add the biscuits and serve at once.
Serves 6

BANANA RIPPLE SPLITS

Put chocolate and single cream into a small heavy-based saucepan. Heat very gently, stirring occasionally, until chocolate has melted. Set aside to cool.

Cut each wafer in half and dip the rounded ends into the chocolate sauce, to coat about ½in/1cm from top. Leave on greaseproof paper to set.

Meanwhile, chill 6 shallow serving dishes.

Peel bananas, cut lengthways in half and brush with lemon juice to prevent browning. Arrange 2 banana halves in each serving dish, top with 4 scoops ice cream and drizzle with chocolate sauce.

Pipe or spoon the cream down the side of each dish. Add the wafers and serve at once. **Serves 6**

6oz/175g plain dessert chocolate, broken into pieces
¼ pint/150ml single cream
6 fan wafers
6 small bananas
2tbls lemon juice
24 small scoops raspberry ripple ice cream
¼ pint/150ml whipping cream, lightly whipped

MOULDED RICE CREAM

4oz/100g cream cheese
1oz/25g caster sugar
grated zest and juice of 1
orange
¼ pint/150ml whipping
cream
2 x 15oz/425g cans
creamed rice
5tsp powdered gelatine,
dissolved in 4tbls water
To decorate:
2 kiwi fruit, sliced
6 strawberries, hulled and
sliced

Line the base and sides of an 8in/20cm sandwich tin with cling film.

Beat the cheese with the sugar, orange zest, orange juice and cream until smooth. Stir in the rice, then beat in the dissolved gelatine. Pour the mixture into the prepared tin. Cover and chill for about 1 hour, or until set.

Uncover the rice, turn out on to a serving plate and remove the cling film. Decorate with kiwi fruit and strawberry slices. **Serves 6**

APRICOT CRISP

Melt margarine, icing sugar, syrup and cocoa together in a saucepan, stirring occasionally. Remove from heat and stir in cornflakes and hazelnuts.

Divide the mixture between 2 greased 8in/20cm sandwich tins base-lined with greased greaseproof paper. Press evenly over the base, then leave for about 30 minutes, or until set.

Turn the chocolate layers out of tins and remove lining paper. Reserve 2tbls cream. Fold half the apricots into the remaining cream and spread over 1 chocolate layer. Place the remaining chocolate layer on top.

Arrange the remaining apricots around the edge. Pipe or spoon the reserved cream in the centre, then decorate with hazelnuts. **Serves 6**

4oz/100g margarine, diced
4oz/100g icing sugar
4tbls golden syrup
2tbls cocoa powder
3oz/75g cornflakes
2oz/50g toasted skinned hazelnuts, chopped
Filling and decoration:
14oz/400g can apricot halves, drained and thinly sliced
½ pint/300ml double cream, lightly whipped
toasted skinned hazelnuts

MELON APPETIZER

3 Galia or other small
  melons, halved and
  seeded
3 oranges, peeled and
  segmented
1 grapefruit, peeled and
  segmented
1oz/25g soft light brown
  sugar
4tbls ginger wine
mint leaves, to garnish

Scoop out the melon flesh with a melon baller or teaspoon and place in a bowl. Add the orange and grapefruit segments, then sprinkle with the sugar and wine. Cover and chill until ready to serve.

Snip a zig-zag edge around top of each melon shell with scissors. Cut a sliver of rind from each base so shells will sit steadily. Wrap tightly and chill.

To serve, divide the fruit between the shells and garnish. **Serves 6**

GOUJONS WITH LEMON SAUCE

oil, for deep frying
1¼lb/500g plaice fillets,
  skinned and cut into
  strips
For the batter:
4oz/100g self-raising
  flour, sifted
1tbls oil
1 egg, beaten
salt and black pepper
For the sauce:
1oz/25g butter
1oz/25g plain flour
¼ pint/150ml milk
¼ pint/150ml single
  cream
1 egg yolk
grated zest and juice of
  ½ lemon
2tbls mayonnaise
To garnish:
lemon wedges
parsley sprigs

To make the batter, place flour, oil and egg in a bowl; season, then stir in 3fl oz/85ml water and beat until smooth.

Heat the oil in a deep fat frier to 325F/170C.

Dry fish on absorbent paper. Stir half the strips into the batter. Fry the battered strips, 1-2 at a time, in the hot oil for 2 minutes until pale golden. Drain on absorbent paper. Coat and fry remaining strips in the same way.

To make the sauce, whisk butter, flour and milk together in a saucepan. Bring to the boil, stirring, then simmer for 2 minutes. Remove from heat and stir in cream, egg yolk, lemon zest and juice and mayonnaise. Season to taste.

Reheat oil to 350F/180C. Place all the fried fish in frying basket and deep fry for 1 minute until golden brown. Drain on absorbent paper.

Garnish and serve at once, with the sauce. **Serves 6**

RITZY CHEESE LOG

2 x 5oz/150g packets
  cheese thins or other
  round savoury crackers
5oz/150g cheese spread
  with shrimps
4oz/100g soft smooth
  liver sausage
5oz/150g cheese spread
  with chives
To garnish:
radish slices
watercress sprigs

Sandwich 30 crackers together, in pairs, with half the shrimp cheese spread. Then use half the liver sausage to sandwich all the pairs of crackers together to make a short log.

Make another short log in the same way, using 30 crackers and the remaining shrimp cheese spread and liver sausage.

Place the remaining crackers between 2 sheets of greaseproof paper and crush finely with a rolling pin.

Spread half the chive cheese spread over each log, covering it completely. Roll each log in the crushed crackers to coat the sides. Press cracker crumbs against the ends of each log. Wrap each log in cling film and chill for 1 hour, to firm.

Transfer the logs to a serving plate and garnish. To serve, cut each log diagonally into slices. **Serves 6**

TOMATO CUPS WITH CRAB

6 large tomatoes
½oz/15g margarine
½oz/15g plain flour
¼ pint/150ml milk
½tsp Tabasco sauce
4oz/100g crabmeat,
  defrosted if frozen,
  drained if canned
2tbls single cream
salt and black pepper
1tbls grated Parmesan
  cheese
To garnish:
lemon twists
dill sprigs

Slice the tops off the tomatoes and reserve. Scoop out and discard flesh and seeds, then stand the shells in a greased shallow flameproof dish.

Whisk the margarine, flour and milk together in a saucepan. Bring to boil, stirring, then simmer gently for 2 minutes. Stir in the Tabasco and crabmeat and cook gently for 1 minute. Remove from the heat, stir in the cream and season to taste.

Divide the crab mixture between the tomato shells. Sprinkle with cheese, then cook under a hot grill for about 2 minutes, until lightly browned.

Replace tops, garnish and serve. **Serves 6**

MUSHROOM DIP

Melt the butter in a saucepan. Add the mushrooms and cook gently for 2 minutes. Cool slightly, then purée in a blender with the cheese and lemon juice.

Season the purée, then pour into a serving bowl or 6 individual dishes. Dust with cayenne, cover and chill until ready to serve.

Serve the dip with the prepared vegetables. **Serves 6**

2oz/50g butter
8oz/225g button mushrooms, sliced
4oz/100g cottage cheese with chives
1tbls lemon juice
salt and black pepper
cayenne pepper, for dusting
To serve:
1lb/450g mixed raw vegetables, cut into sticks

CRISPY CHEESE CUBES

1lb/450g St Paulin cheese,
    rind removed and cut
    into cubes
2 eggs, beaten
2oz/50g fresh
    breadcrumbs
oil, for deep frying
coriander sprigs, to
    garnish
relish or chutney, to serve

Turn the cheese cubes, a few at a time, in the beaten egg; lift out with a teaspoon and turn in the breadcrumbs until evenly coated on all sides. Transfer to a plate and chill for 1 hour.

Heat the oil in a deep-fat frier to 380F/195C.

Place half the cheese cubes in the frying basket and deep fry for about 1 minute, until golden brown. Drain on absorbent paper and keep warm while you fry the remaining cubes in the same way as the first batch.

Garnish and serve at once, with relish or chutney. **Serves 6**

PÂTÉ STUFFED EGGS

6 hard-boiled eggs
7oz/200g pâté
salt and black pepper
To garnish:
lettuce leaves
tomato wedges
6 black olives, halved and
    stoned

Cut the eggs in half lengthways.

Place the yolks in a bowl, add the pâté and season to taste, then beat until smoothly blended. Pipe or spoon the mixture into the egg whites.

Arrange the eggs on a plate with the lettuce and garnish with tomato wedges and olives. **Serves 6**

CURRIED PRAWN SCALLOPS

Make up the potato with 1 pint/600ml boiling water, following the instructions on the packet. Beat in ½oz/15g butter and leave to cool.

Meanwhile, melt the remaining butter in a saucepan. Add the onion and fry for 2 minutes, until softened. Stir in the flour, curry powder and tomato purée and cook, stirring, for 1 minute. Pour in the stock and bring to the boil, stirring, then cover and simmer gently for 10 minutes.

While the sauce is cooking, place the potato in a large piping bag fitted with a medium-sized star nozzle and pipe a border around the edges of 6 shallow flameproof dishes. Cook under a hot grill until the potato is golden brown.

Stir the prawns and soured cream into the sauce and heat gently, without boiling. Spoon the mixture into the centre of each dish, garnish and serve.

Serves 6

5¼oz/150g packet instant mashed potato
2oz/50g butter or margarine
1 onion, finely chopped
1½oz/40g plain flour
2tsp curry powder
2tsp tomato purée
¾ pint/450ml chicken stock
12oz/350g peeled prawns, defrosted if frozen
¼ pint/150ml soured cream
To garnish:
6 lemon twists
parsley sprigs

ASPARAGUS SOUP

1lb/450g asparagus spears
1oz/25g butter or
  margarine
1 onion, finely chopped
1oz/25g plain flour
1¼ pints/700ml chicken
  stock
salt and black pepper
¼ pint/150ml single
  cream
croûtons, to garnish

Trim the woody ends off the asparagus. Cut off and reserve the tips, then chop the stems into short lengths.

Melt butter in a saucepan. Add the chopped asparagus and onion and cook gently, stirring occasionally, for 5 minutes.

Add the flour and cook, stirring, for 1 minute, then slowly stir in the stock. Bring to the boil, cover and simmer for 20 minutes.

Cool the soup slightly, then purée in a blender. Return the soup to the pan, add the asparagus tips and simmer gently for 2 minutes. Season to taste.

Stir in the cream and heat through briefly, without boiling. Serve at once, with croûtons. **Serves 6**

VICHYSSOISE

1oz/25g margarine or
  butter
1lb/450g leeks, sliced
2 celery stalks, chopped
1lb/450g floury potatoes,
  diced
1¼ pints/700ml chicken
  stock
½ pint/300ml milk
salt and black pepper
¼ pint/150ml single
  cream

Melt the margarine in a large saucepan. Add the leeks and celery and cook for 3 minutes until soft but not brown. Add the potatoes and pour in the stock. Bring to the boil, cover and simmer gently for 20 minutes.

Cool the soup slightly, then purée in a blender until smooth. Pour into a bowl and allow to cool, then stir in the milk and season to taste. Cover and chill for 1-2 hours.

To serve, ladle the soup into individual bowls and add a swirl of cream. **Serves 6**

MIXED LEAF SALAD

½ endive
2 heads chicory
2 radicchio (Italian red-
  leaved chicory)
½ Chinese cabbage
  (optional)
1 bunch watercress
For the dressing:
6tbls oil
2tbls wine vinegar
½tsp Dijon mustard
1 garlic clove, crushed
1tsp soft light brown sugar
salt and black pepper

Separate the endive, chicory and radicchio into leaves. Shred the cabbage, if using. Arrange the leaves with the watercress on a serving plate.

To make the dressing, pour the oil and vinegar into a small bowl. Add the mustard, garlic and sugar and season to taste, then whisk with a fork until well blended. Pour into a small jug.

Serve the salad with the dressing handed separately. **Serves 6**

VEGETABLES AU GRATIN

Cook the celery in boiling salted water for about 5 minutes, or until almost tender, then drain. Arrange the celery and artichoke slices over the base of a buttered shallow ovenproof dish. To make the sauce, whisk margarine, flour and milk together in a saucepan. Bring to the boil, stirring, then simmer for 2 minutes. Season and pour over the vegetables.

For the topping, melt the butter in a frying pan, add the breadcrumbs and fry until golden. Stir the breadcrumbs into the cheese, then sprinkle evenly over the sauce.

Bake in the oven preheated to 350F/ 180C/Gas 4 for about 20 minutes, or until topping is crisp and vegetables are tender. Garnish with celery slices and leaves and serve. **Serves 4-6**

1 celery heart, sliced
salt
14oz/400g can artichoke hearts, drained and sliced
For the sauce:
1oz/25g margarine
1oz/25g plain flour
½ pint/300ml milk
black pepper
For the topping:
4oz/100g butter or margarine
6oz/175g fresh white breadcrumbs
4oz/100g Cheddar cheese, finely grated
To garnish:
a few celery slices
celery leaves

CAULIFLOWER SPECIAL

1 cauliflower
1lb/450g broccoli spears
salt
2oz/50g butter or
   margarine
1oz/25g fresh
   breadcrumbs
yolks of 2 hard-boiled eggs
1 tbls finely chopped
   parsley

Trim the cauliflower and broccoli, cutting away the thick stalks, then break into florets. Cook in boiling salted water for about 4 minutes, or until just tender, then drain.

Arrange the broccoli around the edge of a warmed serving dish, then place the cauliflower in the centre. Keep warm.

Melt the butter in a frying pan, add the breadcrumbs and fry until golden brown. Remove from the heat.

Rub the egg yolks through a coarse nylon sieve, then stir into the breadcrumbs with the parsley.

Sprinkle the egg and breadcrumb mixture over the cauliflower and serve at once. **Serves 6**

FENNEL IN TOMATO SAUCE

1 tbls oil
2 onions, finely chopped
1 garlic clove, crushed
4 tomatoes, skinned,
   seeded and chopped
1 tbls tomato purée
salt and black pepper
1 large fennel, trimmed
   and separated into
   leaves
fennel sprigs, to garnish

Heat the oil in a saucepan. Add the onion and fry until softened. Stir in the garlic, chopped tomatoes and tomato purée. Season to taste and simmer for 5 minutes.

Meanwhile, cut each fennel leaf lengthways in half and cook in boiling salted water for about 4 minutes, or until tender, then drain.

Arrange the fennel leaves in a warmed serving dish. Spoon over the tomato sauce, garnish and serve.
Serves 6

CUCUMBERS IN CREAM

2 cucumbers
salt
dill sprigs, to garnish
For the sauce:
¾oz/20g margarine
¾oz/20g plain flour
½ pint/300ml milk
1 bay leaf
2tsp finely chopped dill
4tbls single cream
black pepper

Cut each cucumber lengthways in half, then scrape out the seeds with a teaspoon.

Cut cucumbers into 2½in/6cm lengths, then into thick chunky strips. Cook the cucumber strips in boiling water for 4 minutes or until soft, then drain.

Arrange the cucumber on a warmed serving dish and keep warm.

To make the sauce, whisk the margarine, flour and milk together in a saucepan. Add the bay leaf and bring slowly to the boil, stirring, then simmer gently for 2 minutes. Discard the bay leaf. Stir in the chopped dill and cream, then season to taste.

Pour the sauce over the cucumber. Garnish with dill sprigs and serve at once. **Serves 6**

PINEAPPLE SIDE SALAD

Using a serrated knife, carefully cut out the pineapple flesh, leaving the shells intact. Cut the flesh into small pieces, discarding the tough woody core, and place in a bowl.

Reserve 2 pieces of date. Add the remaining dates to the pineapple pieces with the red pepper and beansprouts.

To make the dressing, stir the allspice into the soured cream.

Pour the dressing over the pineapple mixture and stir gently until well mixed.

Pile the salad into the pineapple shells and garnish with the reserved dates. Serve any remaining salad in a separate bowl. **Serves 6**

1 pineapple, cut in half
  lengthways
2oz/50g stoned dates,
  chopped
1 red pepper, seeded and
  chopped
8oz/225g beansprouts
For the dressing:
1/2tsp ground allspice
1/4 pint/150ml soured
  cream

ROAST RIB OF BEEF

1oz/25g lard
5lb/2.3kg fore rib of beef,
  on the bone
2tbls plain flour
½ pint/300ml hot
  vegetable stock
salt and black pepper
To serve:
cooked vegetables
Yorkshire puddings

Put the lard into a roasting tin and place in the oven preheated to 400F/200C/Gas 6 until melted.

. Place the beef in the tin and baste with the hot fat. Return to the oven and roast for about 1½ hours for rare or 2-2¼ hours for medium to well done, basting from time to time during cooking.

Transfer the beef to a heated serving dish and keep warm.

Stir the flour into the juices in the roasting tin, then slowly stir in the stock. Season to taste and bring to the boil, stirring. Pour the gravy into a sauce-boat.

Serve the beef with the gravy, a choice of vegetables and Yorkshire puddings. **Serves 6**

YORKSHIRE PUDDINGS

4oz/100g plain flour
salt and black pepper
2 eggs
¼ pint/150ml milk
a little lard

Sift the flour into a mixing bowl and season to taste. Make a well in the centre, add the eggs and half the milk and beat with a wooden spoon until smooth. Gradually beat in the remaining milk and ¼ pint/150ml water to make a smooth batter.

Dot 12 bun tins with lard, then place above the centre of the oven preheated to 400F/200C/Gas 6 until hot. Remove from the oven and divide the batter between the tins. Return to the oven and bake for about 30 minutes, or until the puddings are well risen and crisp.

Remove the puddings from the tins and serve at once. **Makes 12**

CHEESE AND HAM SOUFFLÉ

For coating the dish:
*1 tbls fresh white
  breadcrumbs*
*1 tbls grated Parmesan
  cheese*
For the soufflé:
2oz/50g margarine
2oz/50g plain flour
½ pint/300ml milk
salt and black pepper
*2oz/50g cooked ham,
  finely chopped*
*2oz/50g Cheddar cheese,
  finely grated*
*1oz/25g grated Parmesan
  cheese*
3 egg yolks
4 egg whites

Mix the breadcrumbs and Parmesan cheese together, then sprinkle over the base of a lightly greased 2 pint/1.2 litre soufflé dish. Tip and tilt the dish until the base and sides are evenly coated, then tip out any excess.

Whisk the margarine, flour and milk together in a saucepan. Season to taste, then bring slowly to the boil, stirring, and simmer for 1 minute. Remove from the heat and beat in the ham and cheeses. Allow to cool slightly, then beat in the egg yolks.

Whisk the egg whites until they stand in stiff peaks. Using a large metal spoon, gently fold the egg whites into cheese and ham sauce.

Pour mixture into the prepared dish. To give the soufflé a 'top hat' effect, run a metal spoon around the top of the mixture in a circle, about 1½in/4cm from the edge.

Bake in the oven preheated to 350F/180C/Gas 4 for about 40 minutes, or until well risen and golden brown. (Do not open the oven door during the first 30 minutes baking, or the soufflé may sink.) Serve at once, while still puffy.
Serves 4

CIDER BAKED SNAPPER

Wash the fish and dry on absorbent paper, then cut off the fins and gills.

Reserve 2tbls fennel for the stuffing. Scatter the remaining fennel and the tomato slices over the base of a shallow ovenproof dish large enough to hold the fish in a single layer.

To make the stuffing, melt the margarine in a saucepan. Add the onion and reserved chopped fennel and cook for 3 minutes until softened. Stir in the breadcrumbs and dill and season to taste.

Spoon half the stuffing into the cavity of each fish. Lay the fish on top of the fennel and tomatoes in the dish. Pour over the cider and season to taste.

Cover dish with a lid or foil and bake in the oven preheated to 350F/180C/. Gas 4 for about 35 minutes, or until fish is tender and the flesh flakes easily when tested with a fork.

Carefully transfer the fish and a few slices of tomato to a warmed serving dish. Garnish the fish and serve at once, with the cooking liquor and vegetables handed separately. **Serves 4**

2 x 1lb/450g red
  snappers, cleaned
1 small fennel, finely
  chopped
4 tomatoes, skinned and
  sliced
½ pint/150ml medium
  cider
For the stuffing:
1oz/25g margarine
1 onion, finely chopped
1oz/25g fresh
  breadcrumbs
1tsp finely chopped dill
salt and black pepper
To garnish:
dill sprigs
lemon slices
6 black olives

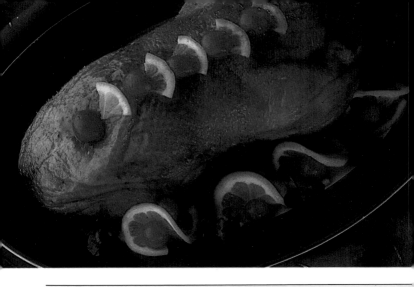

DUCK WITH CHERRIES

4lb/2kg oven-ready duck,
  defrosted if frozen
For the stuffing:
1 tbls oil
1 onion, finely chopped
4oz/100g button
  mushrooms, chopped
grated zest of 1 lemon
4oz/100g fresh white
  breadcrumbs
salt and black pepper
1 egg, beaten
15oz/425g can red
  cherries, drained and
  stoned
For the sauce:
1oz/25g plain flour
½ pint/300ml hot giblet or
  chicken stock
1 tbls clear honey
3 tbls cherry brandy
  (optional)
To garnish:
lemon twists and quarters
watercress sprigs
fresh cherries (optional)

To make the stuffing, heat the oil in a saucepan. Add the onion and mushrooms and fry for 2 minutes. Stir in lemon zest and breadcrumbs and season. Remove from the heat and stir in the beaten egg and half the cherries.

Stuff neck end of duck, then place remaining stuffing in body cavity. Secure neck and tail end of duck with skewers or sew with string. Prick skin all over with a fork or skewer.

Place duck on a rack in a roasting tin. Roast in the oven preheated to 400F/200C/Gas 6 for about 1½ hours, or until juices run clear when meat is pierced with a knife. Pour off excess fat during cooking.

Place duck on a warmed serving dish and remove skewers or string.

To make the sauce, pour off excess fat from roasting tin, then stir the flour into the cooking juices. Stir in the stock and honey. Bring to the boil and simmer, stirring, for 2 minutes. Check the seasoning. Stir in brandy, if using, and remaining cherries.

Pour some of the sauce over the duck. Garnish duck, and serve, with remaining sauce handed separately.
Serves 4-6

PARTY PORK

Place each slice of pork between cling film and beat with a rolling pin to flatten.

Roll out 1 pastry sheet on a lightly floured surface to a 6 x 15in/15 x 38cm rectangle. Cut across in half and brush lightly with egg.

Place a slice of pork on each piece of pastry. Top the pork with an apple slice, a few onion rings and a sage leaf; season, then add ½tbls cream. Fold the pastry over the pork to enclose it completely and seal the joins firmly.

Make 4 more parcels in the same way, using 2 of the remaining pastry sheets, the pork slices, apple rings, onion, sage leaves and cream. Turn the parcels over so the joins are underneath and brush with egg.

Thinly roll out remaining pastry and cut into narrow strips, about 6in/15cm long. Arrange a lattice of strips over each parcel. Trim excess pastry and brush the lattice with egg.

Place the parcels on a baking tray. Bake in the oven preheated to 375F/190C/Gas 5 for about 30 minutes, until the pastry is risen and golden brown. Garnish and serve at once. **Serves 6**

1½lb/700g pork fillet, cut into 6 slices
4 sheets frozen puff pastry, defrosted
1 small egg, beaten
1 cooking apple, cored and cut into 6 rings
1 onion, sliced into rings
6 sage leaves
3tbls single cream
salt and black pepper
To garnish:
apple slices brushed with lemon juice
lemon quarters
sage leaves

GOULASH

4tbls oil
2 onions, thinly sliced
1 garlic clove, crushed
3tbls plain flour
2tbls sweet paprika
salt and black pepper
1½lb/700g braising steak,
    cut into strips
2 x 15oz/425g cans
    tomatoes
1tbls tomato purée
2 bay leaves
2tsp granulated sugar
¼ pint/150ml soured
    cream
To garnish:
bay leaves
triangles of toast

Heat 2tbls oil in a frying pan. Add onions and garlic and fry for 3 minutes. Remove from heat and reserve.

Place flour in a polythene bag. Add paprika and season. Add meat and shake well until evenly coated.

Heat remaining oil in a flameproof 4 pint/2.3 litre casserole. Add meat and fry over high heat until browned on all sides. Stir in any remaining flour, the tomatoes, tomato purée, bay leaves, sugar and fried onions. Bring to the boil, then cover and simmer gently for about 2 hours, until meat is tender.

Remove bay leaves. Stir in soured cream. Garnish and serve. **Serves 6**

STEAK AND MUSHROOM PIE

3tbls oil
2 onions, finely chopped
8oz/225g button
    mushrooms
2tbls plain flour
salt and black pepper
1lb/450g braising steak,
    cut into cubes
½ pint/300ml barley wine
12oz/350g frozen puff
    pastry, defrosted
beaten egg, to glaze

Heat 1tbls oil in a large frying pan. Add the onions and mushrooms and fry for 3 minutes, then set aside.

Place flour in a polythene bag and season. Add meat and shake well.

Fry meat in remaining oil in a large saucepan over high heat until browned on all sides. Add any remaining flour, then stir in the wine and bring to the boil. Add the fried vegetables, cover and simmer gently for about 2 hours, until the meat is tender. Allow to cool.

Roll out half the pastry on a lightly floured surface and use to line an 8in/20cm pie dish. Spoon in the meat mixture. Dampen pastry edge.

Roll out remaining pastry to a 9½in/24cm round. Place over meat filling and press round the edge to seal. Trim, then knock up and flute the edge. Cut a small slit in the top. Use the pastry trimmings to make decorations and arrange on the lid. Brush with egg.

Bake in the oven preheated to 425F/220C/Gas 7 for about 40 minutes, or until the pastry is golden. **Serves 6**

VEAL ESCALOPES MARSALA

4oz/100g button mushrooms, chopped
3oz/75g butter
1 tbls plain flour
1 tsp finely chopped rosemary
2 tbls lemon juice
salt and black pepper
2 tbls single cream
6 slices Italian cured ham
6 veal escalopes, beaten with a mallet to 1/4in/ 5mm thick
2 1/2 fl oz/65ml Marsala or sweet sherry
1/4 pint/150ml chicken stock
1 tbls cornflour
piped potatoes, to serve
To garnish:
rosemary sprigs
4 lemon twists

Fry the mushrooms in 1oz/25g butter for 2 minutes. Stir in flour, rosemary and lemon juice. Season and cook for 1 minute. Stir in the cream, then cool.

Place a slice of ham on each piece of veal, then spread with the mushroom mixture. Roll up firmly and secure with a wooden cocktail stick.

Fry the rolls in the remaining butter for 4 minutes, turning once. Add the Marsala and chicken stock, bring to the boil, cover and simmer for 15 minutes.

Transfer the veal rolls to a warmed serving dish.

Blend cornflour with 2 tbls water and stir into pan juices. Simmer, stirring, for 1 minute, then pour over veal rolls.

Garnish and serve, with potatoes.
Serves 6

HADDOCK ROULADE

Bring margarine, flour and milk slowly to the boil, stirring. Add cottage cheese, spinach and nutmeg, season and cook for 2 minutes. Keep warm.

Mix the haddock, Parmesan cheese, cream and egg yolks together. Whisk the egg whites until stiff, then fold into the haddock mixture.

Pour into a greased 9 x 13in/23 x 33cm Swiss roll tin lined with greased greaseproof paper. Bake, above centre, in the oven preheated to 375F/190C/Gas 5 for 10-15 minutes, until springy to the touch.

Turn out of tin on to a sheet of greaseproof paper. Remove lining paper. Spread with the warm spinach mixture, then roll up from 1 short end with the aid of the paper.

Garnish and serve. **Serves 4-6**

1oz/25g margarine
1oz/25g plain flour
¼ pint/150ml milk
4oz/100g cottage cheese
4oz/100g spinach, cooked and chopped
¼tsp grated nutmeg
salt and black pepper
8oz/225g smoked haddock, cooked and flaked
1tbls grated Parmesan cheese
2tbls single cream
6 eggs, separated
To garnish:
tomato slices and wedges
coriander leaves

CHOCOLATE CREAM PUFFS

2oz/50g margarine
2½oz/65g plain flour,
  sifted
2 eggs, beaten
For the filling:
½ pint/300ml whipping
  cream, lightly whipped
For the sauce:
1oz/25g butter
4tbls golden syrup
4oz/100g plain dessert
  chocolate, broken into
  pieces

To make choux pastry, place margarine in a heavy-based saucepan with ¼ pint/150ml water. Heat gently until the margarine has melted, then bring to the boil.

Quickly remove pan from the heat, tip in all the flour and beat vigorously with a wooden spoon until the mixture leaves the sides of the pan. Beat in the eggs a little at a time. Continue beating until the pastry is smooth and shiny.

Place pastry in a large piping bag fitted with a medium-sized plain nozzle. Pipe about 60 blobs of pastry, slightly apart, on to 2 greased baking trays.

Bake in the oven preheated to 400F/200C/Gas 6 for about 35 minutes, or until the puffs are well risen and golden. Pierce base of each puff, then leave to cool on a wire rack.

Fill the puffs with cream, piping it through the slit in the base. Pile on a serving dish.

To make the sauce, place butter, syrup and chocolate in a heatproof bowl. Set over a pan of hot water until melted, stirring occasionally.

Drizzle some of the warm sauce over the puffs. Serve at once, with the remaining sauce. **Serves 6**

MANGO SORBET

Cut a slice from the top of each orange and reserve for lids. Using a teaspoon, scrape out the orange flesh, keeping the shells intact. Remove any pips. Place the orange flesh in a blender and purée until smooth, then strain into a bowl.

Cut the mango flesh from the stones and purée in the blender. Add to the orange juice with the sugar and stir well. Stir in the dissolved gelatine.

Pour the mixture into a shallow freezer proof container, cover and freeze for about 2 hours or until frozen about 1in/2.5cm around the edges.

Turn the icy mixture into a bowl and whisk thoroughly. Using clean beaters, beat the egg whites until stiff, then whisk into the orange mixture.

Fill each orange shell with the orange sorbet mixture. Place in a freezer proof container, cover and freeze for about 3 hours until firm. Freeze the remaining orange sorbet mixture in a separate container.

Transfer the containers to the refrigerator about 15 minutes before serving, to allow the sorbet to soften. Top each orange with a scoop of the separately frozen sorbet, replace the lids, decorate and serve. **Serves 6**

6 small oranges
2 mangoes
4oz/100g caster sugar
2tsp powdered gelatine,
    dissolved in 3tbls water
2 egg whites
6 mint leaves, to decorate

CHESTNUT CONES

2oz/50g plain flour, sifted
2oz/50g icing sugar
1 egg, separated
2tbls oil
3tbls milk
½tsp vanilla essence
For the filling:
8oz/225g sweetened
  chestnut purée
½ pint/300ml double
  cream, lightly whipped
1oz/25g shelled unsalted
  pistachio nuts, chopped

Line 3 baking sheets with non-stick baking paper. Draw 5 x 3½in/9cm circles on each piece of paper.

Beat the flour, icing sugar, egg yolk, oil, milk and essence together. Whisk the egg white until stiff, then fold into the flour mixture.

Spread about ½tbls of the mixture over each circle. Bake in the oven preheated to 350F/180C/Gas 4 for 5 minutes. Quickly loosen the rounds from the paper with a palette knife, then return to the oven for 3-4 minutes until the edges are pale gold.

Working quickly, roll each round in turn into a cone shape and carefully insert the pointed end in a wire rack. Leave until set and crisp.

For the filling, beat the chestnut purée until smooth, then fold in half the cream. Pipe or spoon the chestnut filling into the cones.

Top each cone with a swirl of the remaining cream and sprinkle with nuts. Serve at once. **Makes 15**

RUM TRUFFLES

8oz/225g plain dessert
  chocolate or chocolate
  cake covering, broken
  into pieces
3oz/75g unsalted butter
  or margarine, diced
2tbls single cream
3tbls dark rum
3oz/75g chocolate
  vermicelli

Place chocolate and butter in a heatproof bowl over a pan of hot, but not boiling, water and leave until melted, stirring occasionally.

Stir the cream and rum into the melted chocolate. Cool, then chill for about 2 hours, or until almost set.

Take 1tsp of the mixture at a time, roll into a small ball, then roll in vermicelli and place on a plate. Continue making truffles until all the mixture is used.

Place the truffles in foil or paper sweet cases. Chill for about 2 hours to firm before serving. **Makes about 30**

COFFEE CHIFFON

2oz/50g butter or
  margarine
2tbls golden syrup
8oz/225g shortbread
  biscuits, crushed
For the filling:
1oz/25g cornflour
2oz/50g granulated sugar
1tbls instant coffee
  granules
½ pint/300ml warm milk
2 eggs, separated
5tsp powdered gelatine,
  dissolved in 4tbls water
½ pint/300ml double
  cream
To decorate:
¼ pint/150ml double
  cream, lightly whipped
coffee beans or chocolate
  buttons

Melt the butter with the syrup in a saucepan over low heat. Remove from the heat and stir in the biscuit crumbs. Press the biscuit mixture evenly over the base of a deep 8in/20cm round cake tin. Cover and chill until required.

To make the filling, mix cornflour, sugar and coffee in a saucepan. Stir in the milk. Bring to the boil, stirring. Beat in egg yolks and cook, stirring, for 2 minutes. Remove from heat and stir in the dissolved gelatine. Leave to cool until thickened but not set.

Whisk the egg whites until stiff. Lightly whip the cream. Fold the cream into the thickened coffee mixture, then fold in the egg whites. Pour over the biscuit base, cover and chill for 3-4 hours until set.

To serve, remove from tin and decorate with piped cream and coffee beans. **Makes 8 slices**

RASPBERRY CHANTILLY

Line 3 baking sheets with non-stick baking paper. Draw 3 x 8in/20cm circles on each.

Whisk egg whites and sugar in a bowl over hot water until thick. Remove from heat and whisk until very stiff.

Place half the meringue in a piping bag fitted with a medium-sized plain nozzle. Pipe a lattice over 1 circle; pipe shells around edge. Spread remaining meringue over other circles and pipe shells around.

Dry out in the oven preheated to 225F/110C/Gas ¼ for about 3 hours, or until crisp. Cool, then lift off paper.

Fold the raspberries into the cream. Layer the meringues with the raspberry cream, ending with the lattice meringue. Decorate with raspberries.

Serves 6-8

4 egg whites
9oz/250g icing sugar, sifted
Filling and decoration:
12oz/350g raspberries, defrosted if frozen
½ pint/300ml double cream, lightly whipped with 1tbls kirsch
extra raspberries

ICED ORANGE SOUFFLÉ

3tbls orange liqueur
1 sachet powdered
 gelatine, dissolved in
 3tbls water
4 eggs, separated
4oz/100g caster sugar
juice of 1 lemon
½ pint/300ml whipping
 cream
For the decoration:
2oz/50g ratafias
¼ pint/150ml whipping
 cream, lightly whipped

Stand a 6in/15cm diameter soufflé dish on a flat plate. Cut a 9 x 20in/ 23 x 50cm strip of greaseproof paper and fold in half lengthways. Wrap the strip around the dish so the paper stands 2in/5cm above the rim and secure with adhesive tape.

Stir the orange liqueur into the dissolved gelatine and keep warm.

Whisk the egg yolks and sugar together until thick and pale. Whisk in the lemon juice.

Using clean beaters, beat the egg whites until stiff. In a separate bowl, whip the cream until it forms soft peaks.

Whisk the dissolved gelatine mixture into the egg yolk and sugar mixture, then quickly fold in the cream. Give the egg whites a brief whisk, then fold into the cream mixture.

Pour the mixture into the prepared soufflé dish and chill for about 1 hour, or until set.

Remove the tape from the paper collar, then carefully peel away from the soufflé with the aid of a round-bladed knife.

Reserve 6-8 ratafias. Coarsely crush the rest and press around the sides of the soufflé. Decorate the top of the soufflé with piped cream and the reserved whole ratafias. **Serves 6-8**

ICED COFFEE

Dissolve the coffee and sugar in 3tbls boiling water in a heatproof jug. Slowly stir in the milk. Cover and chill for at least 1 hour.

Pour the iced coffee into a chilled serving jug.

Whip the cream until thickened, but not too stiff to pour. Slowly pour the cream on the surface of the coffee. Sprinkle with grated chocolate and serve at once. **Serves 6**

2tbls instant coffee granules
1tbls caster sugar
1½ pints/850ml milk
½ pint/150ml whipping cream
1tsp grated plain dessert chocolate

SPECIAL OCCASIONS

FLORIDA SPARKLE

juice of ½ grapefruit
juice of 1 orange
soda water
a little finely shredded
    orange zest, to decorate

Pour the fruit juices into a tall glass. Fill to the top with soda water. Sprinkle with orange shreds and serve at once.
Serves 1

LOVING TOAST

2 large slices white bread
butter, for spreading

Cut the bread into hearts, or other shapes, using a biscuit cutter. Toast the shapes on each side under a hot grill until golden.

Spread with butter and serve at once.
Serves 1

MOTHER'S DAY EGGS

½oz/15g butter or
    margarine
2 eggs
2tbls milk
salt and black pepper
To garnish:
4 small bacon rolls, grilled
3 tomato wedges
parsley sprig

Melt the butter in a small non-stick saucepan. Beat the eggs with the milk, season and pour into the pan. Cook very gently, stirring constantly, until the egg thickens.

Spoon the scrambled egg on to a warmed serving plate, garnish and serve at once. **Serves 1**

PARTY KEBABS

10 rindless streaky bacon
   rashers
8oz/225g Edam cheese,
   cut into 20 cubes
20 tomato wedges
15oz/425g can baby corn
   on the cob, drained and
   cut in half
5 beefburgers, quartered
10 thin sausages, halved
1lb/450g can pineapple
   cubes, drained
boiled rice, to serve
coriander or parsley
   sprigs, to garnish

Cut the bacon rashers across in half, then wrap each piece around a cube of cheese.

Thread a tomato wedge on to each of 10 kebab skewers, followed by a cube of bacon wrapped cheese, a piece of corn, beefburger and sausage and a pineapple cube. Add the remaining ingredients in the same order as before but adding the tomato wedges at the end.

Cook the kebabs under a moderate grill for about 8 minutes, turning once, or until the meat is cooked through.

Serve on a bed of rice, garnished with coriander. **Serves 10**

CHOCOLATE MALLOW

Place marshmallows, butter and milk in a saucepan and heat gently, stirring occasionally, until melted.

Stir in the crushed biscuits, then divide between 10 small dessert glasses. Reserve.

Stir the egg yolks and sherry into the melted chocolate and leave until cool.

Whisk the egg whites until stiff, then fold into the chocolate mixture. Divide the mixture between the glasses, covering the biscuit base. Cover and chill for 2 hours.

For the decoration, dip each marshmallow into the melted chocolate, then leave on greaseproof paper to set.

Just before serving, top each dessert with 1tbls spooning cream and a chocolate marshmallow. **Serves 10**

8oz/225g marshmallows
4oz/100g butter or
  margarine, diced
4tbls milk
1lb/450g shortbread
  biscuits, finely crushed
4 eggs, separated
4tbls sherry
6oz/175g plain dessert
  chocolate, melted
To decorate:
10 marshmallows
1oz/25g plain dessert
  chocolate, melted
½ pint/300ml spooning
  cream

ALMOND KISSES

4oz/100g ground almonds
2oz/50g cornflour
1tsp almond essence
5oz/150g caster sugar
3 egg whites
Filling and decoration:
6oz/170g can sterilised
    cream
4oz/100g plain dessert
    chocolate, broken into
    pieces

Mix the almonds with the cornflour, essence and 2oz/50g sugar.

Whisk the egg whites until stiff, then whisk in the remaining sugar, 1tsp at a time. Fold in the almond mixture.

Place the mixture in a large piping bag fitted with a small star nozzle and pipe about 60 tiny shells on to 2 baking sheets lined with non-stick baking paper.

Bake in the oven preheated to 325F/160C/Gas 3 for about 25 minutes, or until the shells lift off the paper easily. Cool on a wire rack.

Warm the cream with the chocolate in a small saucepan, stirring occasionally until the chocolate is melted. Pour half the chocolate cream into a bowl, cover and chill until thick. Reserve remaining chocolate cream.

Sandwich the shells together in pairs with the chilled chocolate cream. Dip tapered end of each pair into the reserved chocolate cream and leave on greaseproof paper to set. **Makes 30**

CHEESE SAVOURIES

8oz/225g self-raising
    flour
½tsp salt
¼tsp mustard powder
2oz/50g margarine, diced
3oz/75g Cheddar cheese,
    finely grated
1 egg, beaten
5tbls milk
5oz/150g cheese spread
    with pineapple
To garnish:
8 radishes, thinly sliced
4oz/100g peeled prawns,
    defrosted if frozen
parsley sprigs

Sift flour, salt and mustard into a bowl. Rub in the margarine. Using a fork, stir in the cheese, egg and milk and mix to a soft dough.

Turn out on to a floured surface and knead lightly. Roll out until ½in/1cm thick. Cut into as many rounds as possible with a 1½in/3.5cm cutter. Knead the trimmings lightly together, roll out again and cut into more rounds to make a total of about 35.

Place on 2 floured baking sheets. Bake in the oven preheated to 400F/200C/Gas 6 for about 15 minutes, until risen and golden. Cool on a wire rack.

To serve, cut in half, spread with cheese spread and garnish. **Makes 70**

CHRISTENING CUP

Place the peach and kiwi fruit slices in a glass serving bowl with the brandy.

Pour in the wine and soda, add 10-12 ice cubes and stir well. Float a few mint leaves on top and serve at once.

Serves 15

8oz/225g can sliced peaches, drained
1 kiwi fruit, sliced
4tbls brandy
2 x 1¼ pint/70cl bottles sparkling white wine, chilled
18fl oz/500ml soda water
mint leaves, to garnish

PRALINE PRINCESS

3oz/75g granulated sugar
3oz/75g blanched almonds
1oz/25g ratafias, finely crushed
4oz/100g meringue shells, crushed
1 pint/600ml double cream, lightly whipped
For the sauce:
1lb/450g raspberries, defrosted if frozen
2-3tbls icing sugar, sifted

Heat the granulated sugar with ¼ pint/150ml water in a heavy-based saucepan, stirring until dissolved. Bring to the boil and boil briskly until the syrup begins to turn pale golden. Add the almonds and cook, shaking the pan until golden. Remove from the heat.

Lift out 10 almonds with a teaspoon and place, apart, on a piece of oiled foil. Pour remaining almonds on to oiled foil; leave until cold, then crush finely to make the praline.

Coat a buttered 1½ pint/850ml freezer proof mould with the ratafias.

Fold the crushed meringues and praline into three-quarters of the cream. Pour into the mould, cover and freeze for 3 hours.

Reserve some of the raspberries. Purée the rest in a blender, sieve into a jug and sweeten to taste, then chill.

Just before serving, dip the mould into warm water, then invert on to a serving plate and lift away from the dessert. Decorate with the remaining cream, the reserved raspberries and almonds. Serve at once, with the chilled raspberry sauce. **Serves 6**

CELEBRATION SALAD

Mix the mayonnaise, tomato purée, cream, onion and ½tbls parsley together until blended. Flake the tuna and fold into the mayonnaise with the prawns.

Cut the mackerel fillets in half lengthways, then cut each half diagonally into thin slices. Reserve 6 slices. Fold the rest into the mayonnaise mixture.

Arrange the lettuce leaves and endive on a serving plate. Pile the fish mayonnaise in centre and sprinkle with the remaining parsley.

Cut the salmon into 6 strips. Cut the herrings into 6 slices. Arrange around the fish mayonnaise with the reserved mackerel slices and king prawns. Garnish and serve. **Serves 6**

¼ pint/150ml
  mayonnaise
1tbls tomato purée
2tbls double cream
1tsp grated onion
1tbls finely chopped
  parsley
7oz/200g can tuna,
  drained
6oz/200g peeled prawns,
  defrosted if frozen
4 smoked mackerel fillets,
  skinned
12 lettuce leaves
¼ endive
3 slices smoked salmon
2 rollmop herrings
6 king prawns, tails
  peeled
To garnish:
tomato wedges
lemon wedges

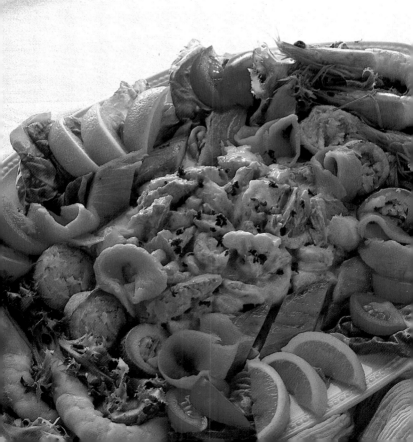

EASTER LAMB

2 best ends neck of lamb
  with 7 cutlets each,
  chined
melted lard
For the stuffing:
3oz/75g rindless streaky
  bacon, chopped
1 onion, finely chopped
1 tbls oil
3oz/75g fresh
  breadcrumbs
1 tbls finely chopped mint
grated zest of 1 lemon
1 egg, beaten
1 tbls milk
salt and black pepper
To garnish:
8oz/225g cocktail cherries
8 lemon twists
mint sprigs

Cut across the top of each joint, about 1in/2.5cm from top of bones. Remove the fat and meat between, leaving the top of the bones clean. Score the fat.

Stand the joints close together, fat sides outside and the exposed bones interlocking. Sew either end together at the base and tie the end bones together with the fine string. Place in a roasting tin and brush with lard.

Make the stuffing: fry the bacon and onion in the oil for 2 minutes, then stir in the breadcrumbs, mint, lemon zest, egg and milk and season.

Fill centre of joint with the stuffing. Roast in the oven preheated to 375F/190C/Gas 5 for 1½ hours, or until the meat is cooked to taste.

Remove the string, place joint on a warmed serving plate and garnish.
Serves 6-8

CHOCOLATE NESTS

4oz/100g self-raising
  flour
1 tsp baking powder
1 tbls cocoa powder
4oz/100g caster sugar
4oz/100g margarine or
  butter, softened
2 eggs
For the icing:
6oz/175g icing sugar,
  sifted
3oz/75g margarine or
  butter, softened
1 tbls cocoa powder,
  dissolved in 1 tbls hot
  water
To finish:
4oz/100g plain dessert
  chocolate, grated
2 shredded wheat, crushed
15 small sugar eggs

Sift flour, baking powder and cocoa into a mixing bowl. Add the sugar, margarine and eggs and beat together with a wooden spoon for 2 minutes.

Divide the mixture between 15 well greased bun tins. Bake in the oven preheated to 350F/180C/Gas 4 for 25 minutes, or until springy to the touch. Turn out and cool on a wire rack.

Using a 1½in/3.5cm plain cutter, hollow out centre of each bun, without cutting through the base, to make 'nests'.

To make the icing, beat the icing sugar and margarine until smooth, then beat in the cocoa.

Spread the outside of each nest with icing, then sprinkle with chocolate.

Fill the centre of each nest with crushed shredded wheat and a sugar egg. **Makes 15**

ANNIVERSARY AVOCADO

1 avocado
2 tsp lemon juice
2 tbls mayonnaise
1 tsp tomato purée
1 tsp finely chopped chives
1 hard-boiled egg, sliced
14 peeled prawns,
    defrosted if frozen
To garnish:
2 lemon twists
dill sprigs

Halve and stone the avocado, then brush the cut surfaces with lemon juice to prevent them browning.

Mix the mayonnaise, tomato purée and chives until evenly blended.

Reserve 4 slices of egg. Chop the rest and stir into the mayonnaise mixture.

Divide the egg mayonnaise between the avocados and top with the reserved egg slices and prawns. Place on serving dishes and garnish with lemon twists and dill sprigs. **Serves 2**

POUSSINS VERONIQUE

Melt the butter in large, deep frying pan. Add the poussins and fry until lightly browned on all sides. Pour in the wine and chicken stock, season and bring to the boil. Cover and simmer for 30 minutes, or until the poussins are tender and the juices run clear when the meat is pierced with a sharp knife.

Transfer the poussins to a warmed serving dish and keep warm.

Blend the cornflour with 2tbls water and stir into the cooking liquid. Bring slowly to the boil, stirring, then simmer for 2 minutes. Remove from the heat and stir in the cream. Check the seasoning.

Pour the sauce over the poussins. Garnish with the grapes and dill and serve at once. **Serves 2**

2oz/50g butter
2 x 1lb/450g oven-ready
  poussins, defrosted if
  frozen
2½fl oz/65ml white wine
¼ pint/150ml chicken
  stock
salt and black pepper
1tbls cornflour
2tbls single cream
To garnish:
4oz/100g mixed black and
  white grapes, halved
  and seeded
dill sprigs

CHRISTMAS TURKEY

10lb/4.5kg oven-ready
 turkey, defrosted if
 frozen
melted lard
6 rindless streaky bacon
 rashers
watercress, to garnish
For the stuffing:
2 onions, finely chopped
2 tbls oil
6oz/175g fresh
 breadcrumbs
2 tbls finely chopped
 parsley
1 tbls finely chopped thyme
grated zest of 1 orange
8fl oz/250ml milk
1lb/450g pork
 sausagemeat
4oz/100g cranberries,
 cooked
salt and black pepper
For the gravy:
2 tbls plain flour

To make the stuffing, fry the onions in
the oil until softened. Remove from
heat and stir in breadcrumbs, herbs,
orange zest and milk. Add sausagemeat
and cranberries, season and mix well.

Stuff neck end of turkey, then spoon
remaining stuffing into the body cavity.
Sew flap of neck skin in place, then tie
up the drumsticks and parson's nose
with fine string.

Place turkey in a large roasting tin
and brush with lard. Cover breast and
neck end with bacon slices. Roast in
the oven preheated to 375F/190C/Gas 5
for about 3¼ hours or until the juices
run clear, basting regularly.

Remove bacon and string. Place
turkey on a warmed serving dish and
garnish.

For the gravy, pour off most of the fat
from the tin, retaining the cooking
juices. Blend the flour into the cooking
juices. Bring to the boil, stirring, and
cook for 2 minutes. Season, then pour
into a sauce-boat.

Serve the turkey at once,
with the gravy. **Serves 10**

CRANBERRY ORANGE CUPS

Cut the oranges in half with a small serrated knife. Cut around the edge of the flesh, then cut between the membrane to free the segments. Lift out the segments and remove any pips.

Scrape the orange shells clean, then mark the edge of each shell into 5 equal sections. Cut a semi-circle from each section with small scissors, to scallop the edge of each shell.

Place the sugar in a saucepan with 2fl oz/50ml water and stir over low heat until dissolved. Add the cranberries, bring to the boil, cover and simmer until the berries stop popping. Remove from the heat and stir in the orange segments. Divide the mixture between the orange shells. **Makes 6**

3 oranges
2oz/50g granulated sugar
3oz/75g cranberries

FESTIVE PUDDING

2oz/50g butter, diced
3tbls golden syrup
1½ x 7oz/200g packets
    crunchy oat biscuits,
    finely crushed
3oz/75g plain dessert
    chocolate, broken in
    pieces
¾ pint/450ml milk
2oz/50g caster sugar
3 egg yolks
1 sachet powdered
    gelatine, dissolved in
    2tbls dark rum
½ pint/300ml whipping
    cream, lightly whipped
assorted glacé cherries,
    halved and chopped, to
    decorate

Line a 1½ pint/850ml pudding basin with foil..

Melt butter and syrup in a saucepan, then stir in the crushed biscuits. Spoon into the lined basin and press evenly over the base and up sides. Chill.

Heat chocolate, milk and sugar in a saucepan, stirring until chocolate has melted. Bring slowly to the boil. Add egg yolks and cook gently, stirring, for 1 minute. Cool slightly, then stir in the dissolved gelatine and rum. Cool, then chill for about 30 minutes until thick but not set.

Fold half the cream into chocolate mixture. Pour into prepared basin. Cover and chill for 3 hours, or until set.

Invert pudding on to a serving dish, lift off basin and remove foil. Cover pudding with the remaining cream and decorate. Chill until ready to serve.
Serves 6-8

ROSY MINCE PIES

12oz/350g shortcrust
    pastry, defrosted if
    frozen
15 maraschino flavour
    cocktail cherries,
    halved
12oz/350g mincemeat
maraschino cherry syrup
    (from the jar), for
    glazing
sifted icing sugar, for
    dredging

Thinly roll out two-thirds of the pastry on a lightly floured surface. Cut into 15 rounds with a 3in/8cm fluted cutter, re-rolling the trimmings as necessary.

Use the rounds to line 15 tart tins and prick each base with a fork. Divide the cherries and mincemeat between the pastry cases. Brush edges with water.

Roll out the remaining pastry and cut into 15 rounds with a 2½in/6.5cm fluted cutter. Place on top of the pastry cases and press edges together to seal. Pierce the top of each lid, then brush generously with cherry syrup.

Bake in the oven preheated to 400F/200C/Gas 6 for about 15 minutes, or until golden. Cool the pies on a wire rack, then dredge with icing sugar.
Makes 15

BLACK BUN

10oz/280g packet white
bread mix
For the filling:
1lb/450g mixed dried fruit
1oz/25g cut mixed peel
2oz/50g glacé cherries,
   chopped
2oz/50g blanched
   almonds, chopped
grated zest of 1 orange
1oz/25g caster sugar
4oz/100g plain flour,
   sifted
1 tsp ground allspice
4oz/100g butter, melted
2 eggs, beaten

Place bread mix in a bowl, add 6½fl oz/
185ml hand-hot water and mix to a
dough. Turn out on to a floured surface
and knead for 5 minutes, then place in
a polythene bag and reserve.

Place the dried fruit, peel, cherries,
almonds, orange zest, sugar, flour and
spice in a mixing bowl and mix well.
Stir in the butter and two-thirds of the
beaten egg.

Cut off and reserve a small piece of
dough. Roll out the remaining dough
on a floured surface to a 12in/30cm
circle. Spoon fruit mixture in centre,
shaping it into a round. Bring the edges
of the dough over the fruit, to enclose
it, and press firmly together to seal.

Turn the bun over and place, seam
side down, on a greased baking sheet.
Prick the top and sides, making sure to
pierce through to the filling. Brush
with most of the remaining egg. Make
decorations from the reserved dough,
place on the bun and brush with egg.

Bake in the oven preheated to 350F/
180C/Gas 4 for 1 hour, or until golden
brown. Cool on a wire rack. **Serves 8**

HIGHLAND FLING

Line the base of a grill pan with foil. Sprinkle the oatmeal over the base, then cook under a medium grill, stirring frequently until golden brown. Set aside to cool.

Whip the cream with the honey and whisky until it forms soft peaks. Fold in the toasted oatmeal.

Divide the mixture between 8 small serving glasses. Cover and chill until required.

Just before serving, top each dessert with a few raspberries. **Serves 8**

2oz/50g medium oatmeal
½ pint/300ml double
* cream*
2tbls clear honey
4tbls Scotch whisky
8oz/225g raspberries,
* defrosted if frozen*

INDEX